Wings to Fly

written by **LYDIA WALLIS**
illustrated by **AMANDA LE**

Text Copyright ©2023 by Lydia Wallis
Illustration Copyright ©2023 by Amanda Le

Think Ahead Kids Publishing

29910 Murrieta Hot Springs Rd. Suite G226 Murrieta, CA 92563

All rights reserved. No part of this publication may be reproduced, stored in a retrieval system, or transmitted in mechanical, photocopying, recording, or otherwise, without the prior written permission of the copyright owner.

Library of Congress Cataloging-in-Publication Data on file.

ISBN 979-8-218-28820-4

Visit ThinkAheadKids.com

*To my little sister Hannah,
who always tries again and again
until she gets it right.*

Once there was a bird named Little Hannah who lived in a small forest.

Her biggest wish was that she could fly.

Most nights her eyes hurt from looking at the sky for so long!

Every time Little Hannah looked at the sky, she thought, *Oh how fun it must be to fly in the great big sky!*

Then, she would stretch her wings and imagine she was flying. She wouldn't really fly because she didn't know how.

One morning,

Little Hannah woke up, stretched her wings, ate some seeds,

and looked down at the ground.

She really wanted to learn how to fly!

She hopped down through the branches to find a forest friend who could teach her.

As she hopped through the forest, she heard a RAT-A-TAT-TAT!

Her friend Mr. Woodpecker was up in a pine tree.

"Hello, Mr. Woodpecker!" she called up.

"I really want to learn how to fly. Can you please teach me how?"

Mr. Woodpecker pulled his beak out of the tree trunk and said,

"I'm sorry Little Hannah, but I am very busy right now. Maybe you can come back tomorrow."

Then he went back to his pecking.

Little Hannah remained hopeful and kept walking.

Soon she arrived at a pond. Mrs. Heron stood by the water, dipping in her head to catch some fish for lunch.

"Hello, Mrs. Heron!" Little Hannah said.

"I have seen you fly before, and you do it beautifully. I was wondering if you could please teach me how to fly like you."

Mrs. Heron took her head out of the water.

"Hi, Little Hannah. I would like to help you, but I'm a little busy gathering food for my family. Maybe next time."

She stuck her head back into the water.

Little Hannah felt
a little disappointed.
She was not sure a friend could
teach her how to fly after all!

Can I do it? she wondered.

Learning how to fly was very important to her,
so she decided to trust herself
and her beautiful wings to do the job.

The only way to find out is to try!

So,

she spread her wings very wide,

closed her eyes,

and took a deep breath.

She felt herself getting braver and braver.

First, she flapped her wings slowly
and then faster and faster.
She opened her eyes. Nothing had happened.

She tried again. Nothing happened.

This went on two more times, but she kept trying.

Then she heard a cheer.

Little Hannah opened her eyes and saw her friends smiling.

"You are flying!" they cheered.

She sure was flying high above the ground!

Little Hannah felt so happy and proud
for trying something so hard.
Now she felt free and knew that if she tried hard,
she could learn to do anything.

Meet the Author

Lydia Wallis lives in Southern California with her mother, father, two younger sisters, and their two Holland Lop rabbits. In her free time, Lydia enjoys reading, writing novels, listening to Taylor Swift, hiking, bird watching, and spending time with her family and friends.

Meet the Illustrator

Amanda Le is an Asian-American artist local to Southern Califonia. They are a life-long lover of stories and art, and creates art that focuses on kindness and art as healing.

They earned a BA in Art and a Masters in Education from UC Irvine. Amanda designed a BIBA Award-winning book cover for poetry anthology "A Burning Lake of Paper Suns," and has done cover work for Spillway Magazine. Just like Little Hannah, Amanda worked hard to achieve their dreams and became a full-time book illustrator in 2023.

ACKNOWLEDGEMENTS

Think Ahead Kids Foundation
would like to Thank:
Bella Allure Salon
Starbucks Foundation
Mercedes Benz of Temecula
Islands Burgers of Temecula
Mountain Mike's Pizza of Temecula
Ronald H. Roberts Temecula Public Library
Paul Roberts, Art by Paul Roberts
Cactus Nutrition Spot Murrieta
Joseph Hart, Reptile Hunter
The Crafthouse of Temecula
Kahoots Temecula
Roripaugh Ranch
Young Smiles
and our editor, Victoria Maldonado

for making this book possible.

THANK YOU!!!

www.ingramcontent.com/pod-product-compliance
Lightning Source LLC
LaVergne TN
LVHW070435080526
838201LV00132B/277